BOUNCE BACK

CHOOSING TO RISE WHEN LIFE KNOCKS YOU DOWN

DR. CHUCK SANDSTROM

Body and Soul Publishing

P.O. Box 6542

Colorado Springs, CO 80934

Bounce Back / Dr. Chuck Sandstrom. -- 1st ed.

ISBN: 978-1-946118-27-1

CONTENTS

CHAPTER 1

GETTING KNOCKED DOWN

"Sometimes, you have to get knocked down lower than you have ever been to stand back up taller than you ever were." - Unknown

On July 1, 2009, my life changed forever. One day, I was the executive director of a community foundation and a civic leader. The next day, I was in a coma in the ICU.

While I was having an unregistered car towed from a rental property I owned in Akron, Ohio, I encountered the owner of the car, Michael. He was drunk and angry. He punched me in the face. My head hit a brick wall a few inches behind me at the speed of a high-speed car wreck. My nose was broken and I knocked out my two front teeth.

I almost died and was unconscious for around six weeks. I have what is called a severe traumatic brain injury or a TBI.

Because of the injury to my brain, I can't remember anything about the assault or anything that happened initially. I really don't know about it at all. And that probably is a gift that God has given to me.

I had been in several situations in that neighborhood, but never felt I had a cause for fear.

The Criminal Case

There were detectives on the case and they activated the fugitive task force, which means there were U.S. Marshals looking for Michael as well. There was a warrant for his arrest and witnesses to the crime. Crime Stoppers also had a reward for information leading to his arrest.

Michael went into hiding the night of the assault and was nearly drinking himself to death. He was hiding from U.S. Marshals, who were prepared to shoot him upon arrest.

He was a fugitive for 15 months before his arrest.

The Results

Recovery has been a slow and difficult journey. My heart broke wide open. I became an outsider to the mainstream life I had known.

But the surprising thing about the assault that ended my life as I knew it is that I lived through it.

Choosing to Rise

We have all been through difficult circumstances in our lives.

Where have you been "knocked down" in your life? Take a few minutes to journal about it.

CHAPTER 2

THE BOUNCE BACK MINDSET

"I can be changed by what happens to me. But I refuse to be reduced by it." - Maya Angelou

Everyone faces adversity during their lifetime. Some face more than others, but each time we come through a setback, we develop more resilience. Each trial is an opportunity to build mental and emotional muscle.

What is a bounce back mindset? It is the ability to effectively cope with and bounce back from setbacks, obstacles, trauma, or difficult situations.

Athletes who suffer injuries must choose to undertake the arduous process of rehab with a positive attitude. Those who fall victim to a natural disaster such as hurricanes, tornados, fires, or earthquakes understand the need to slowly pick up the pieces and move forward.

No matter what setback you face, you can choose your mindset. Here are three mindsets that have helped me to bounce back.

Faith: Choosing to Believe the Impossible

One of the staff members at the nursing home where I stayed said she had heard about the amazing progress I was making. She said I was the "talk of the building" with all the other staff as they followed my progress.

She said she had not seen any "miracles" for a while and had given up believing. But she said after seeing the progress I made, she thinks she believes in miracles again!

She said, "I know that I only clean your room, but in doing that, I feel a part of something so much bigger, so much greater." She had a renewed sense of purpose in her as she talked.

God is at work and I am thankful to God for the miracles we see every day.

For a season, I even had my own business and was a motivational speaker. The guy with a speech impairment made his living…wait for it…speaking! It's funny, but it's true.

I want people to know that they can accomplish something greater than they ever imagined. I can imagine greatness for everyone. By the way, greatness does not just happen inside professional sports arenas or on music stages with large audiences.

Ordinary people all over the world are doing extraordinary things that few people will ever see. Serving at homeless shelters, working the night shift in an ER, setting up and tearing down for church services week after week, and teachers pouring their lives into troubled students are just a few examples of these unsung heroes doing great things.

Perseverance: Willingness to Do the Work

I do not take the simple miracle of being alive for granted.

I came out of therapy and knew I wanted to do more. Traditional medicine and therapy said this is as good as you're going to get. You are going to be in a wheelchair. But I decided I wanted to be better. I wanted to be as good or better than I was before.

Having this mindset has helped me to persevere in the healing process. I have always been a go-getter and high achiever and I brought that mindset into my recovery.

My personal trainer told me, "Chuck, you don't have a disability. The only thing you have is just a different type of roadblock that we have to learn to go around."

Gratitude: Focusing on What You Have Instead of What You Lost

After the assault, I lost what many would call everything - job, new home, property, finances, and social standing.

However, having a positive attitude has been my hallmark. I feel good no matter the circumstances. I have a positive mental attitude. PMA.

I have kept my sense of humor and laugh at everything. If anyone is a comedian, it's good to have me around. I always look at a stranger as a friend I haven't met yet.

We can focus on what we don't have or be grateful for what we do have. As my daughter Stacey used to say to my granddaughters when they were young, "You get what you get and you don't throw a fit. You get what you get and be grateful for it."

Although I talk funny and walk funny, I am grateful to be ALIVE.

Will You Choose a Bounce Back Mindset?

I was a man who used to work with people who were trying to accomplish something great. Something great, like raising a million dollars to build a new facility or transform an organization.

Now I'm a man who wants to help people like you accomplish something great. For example, rising out of wheelchairs, financial, emotional, and physical devastation, and fighting to create a worthwhile life.

Will you join me?

Choosing to Rise

Viktor Frankl was a man who had experienced being knocked down. In 1942, he and his family were sent to Nazi concentration camps. While in these camps, Frankl lost his father, mother, brother, and finally his beloved wife. Viktor himself survived three years in four different concentration camps during the Holocaust.

Writing numerous books, including the popular *Man's Search for Meaning*, it would be an understatement to say that Viktor Frankl had a bounce back mindset. In one of his more famous quotes regarding our response to what life throws at us, he says,

"Between stimulus and response, there is space. In that space is our power to choose our response. In our response lies our growth and our freedom."

What has been your most common response to the "stimulus" of things thrown at you throughout your life? What role has gratitude played in your life? Take a few minutes to journal about it. Also, write out five things you are grateful for today.

CHAPTER 3

CHOOSING TO STAND BACK UP

"The greatest glory in living lies not in never falling, but in rising every time we fall." - Nelson Mandela

I want to share a timeline that highlights some of the progress I made following my brain injury.

Little by Little

After the assault, it was three weeks before I was able to open my eyes on command. The next day after that, I was able to turn my head at the sound of a voice. It would then be another three weeks before I finally emerged from the coma on August 13th, 2009.

The whole place was filled with joyful hospital staff coming in to say hello and I was able to acknowledge them all. At one point, twelve nurses and aides gathered in and out of my room, crying and cheering!

On September 1st, I was able to ditch my walker. My physical therapist nearly cried and said, "Oh my, Chuck. You are going to be our poster child!"

On September 23rd, they discharged me from Edwin Shaw Rehab Hospital. Amazingly, other than my brain injury, I was told my health was perfect and I could live medicine free. I credit the prayers and encouragement of family and friends.

On September 28th, my first trombone lesson went really well even though I was missing my two front teeth. I'm so grateful I've been able to enjoy playing my trombone in various bands throughout my life, before and after my brain injury.

On November 5th, I began swimming at a place called Gilcrest. I also worked with a personal trainer named John. I realized I was the only one who could actually do the work of getting stronger while having someone else help keep me accountable. I had been told that John is a hard-working guy who could help me become younger and stronger as a result of working with him.

Besides John, I also had the privilege of working with another trainer named Troy for several years. I owe these fine men so much for all the ways they pushed me to become better and stronger. Their belief in me gave me the motivation to shed some good old-fashioned blood, sweat and tears in the gym.

One of the first things that I learned how to do was to drive a car. A guy that my physical therapist hired as a driver was taking his life into his own hands by evaluating my driving! But I passed a test with his help and being able to do that has given me independence. For years I drove myself to the gym every morning to workout Monday through Friday.

June 1st, 2010 was a day to celebrate. Not only was I cleared by my doctor to drive, but I also accepted a part-time position at Goodyear Heights Presbyterian Church as an outreach associate. For several years, I visited shut-ins while also participating in other outreach work. I am so grateful for Pastor Christy who gave me this chance to serve in a meaningful way.

Today, I continue to swim, golf, and play my trombone in a local band. I also play a mean game of online Scrabble and have even completed a local 5k race. Staying active has been good for both my mind and body.

I am choosing to stand back up.

Choosing to Rise

In what ways have you chosen to stand back up after getting knocked down in life? Take some time to write out the names of those who have helped you the most in your life. If possible, send each of them a hand-written letter expressing your heartfelt thanks for the ways they helped you get back on your feet.

CHAPTER 4

FORGIVENESS AS A WAY OF LIFE

"Forgiveness is first and foremost a way of seeing. It cannot change the facts about the world we live in but it can change the way we see those facts." - Harold Kushner

On October 11, 2010 I did the unthinkable. I chose to forgive Michael.

I asked Michael's family to pass on the message that I forgave Michael completely, that I liked him, and felt regret for his family.

About three months later, Michael pled guilty on 1/19/2011 to a charge of Felonious Assault, a felony of the 2nd degree. The sentencing guideline for this degree of a crime can range at a minimum of 2 years to a maximum of 8 years. There is a presumption a defendant will receive a prison commitment on this degree of a crime. They gave Michael a 4-year prison commitment.

At sentencing, Michael was asked if he had anything to say before he was sentenced. He said he was sorry for what he had done and the harm he caused me. He told the judge he wanted to take full advantage of the programs offered at the institution to work on his anger/anger management as well as Alcoholics Anonymous meetings to change for the better for when he was released.

When Michael was finally arrested, I realized that seeing him get sentenced, though necessary, would not bring healing. What had helped me the most had been reaching out to his family. It was like being the first ones standing up after an earthquake and wanting to help other hurting people to stand up too. It helped me recover from my pain.

In early 2011, I started helping Michael's family and it was very rewarding for me.

Who among us has not been harmed by the actions of another? Who has not experienced injustice? Who among us has not experienced first or second hand a seemingly senseless tragedy? We can make tragedy make sense when we allow it to help us find our way back to God, to each other, and to a place of love.

There was a moment in the courtroom pretrial when Michael turned and looked my way. Our eyes met. All either of us saw in the other's eyes at that moment was compassion.

Later, when Michael learned I had forgiven him, he didn't know what to do. He told his significant other he had never had such a strange feeling. He felt love like he had never felt it before. It made him want to understand it. He asked for a Bible in jail and started reading it.

I received weekly letters from Michael. He said he found faith in prison and help for his alcoholism. He thanked us constantly for our work with his family and told us of his own progress. I wanted to see him get back to being a good father who provides for his kids and possibly a friend to me. According to statistics, men like him don't change. His future should look like his past: alcohol, rage, bullying and prison.

On 2/14/14, Michael and I met for the first time since the assault.

I was glad to meet with Michael. We were good friends immediately. And I expected to be a great help to him as he would be a help to me as I dealt with my stuff. I am very grateful for Michael and his significant other and any relationship we were able to experience.

The most striking thing about it was how "normal" we were: two families at Cracker Barrel having a meal.

It was between Michael and God regarding what path he would ultimately take in life. My business is what is in my heart. We are each responsible for the actions we choose.

Choosing to Forgive

You might think there's no way you can forgive someone who harmed you. Love the person enough to put yourself in the position that you would want to be in if you committed the act yourself.

Ask God to help you. He will do it. You don't want to miss out on the freedom.

Forgiving one another is one of the main things God asks us to do and He supplies the power to do it. Forgiveness is the work Christ specifically asked us to do.

Forgiveness is practical. Forgiveness is liberating. Forgiveness is an attitude that can be learned, and forgiveness can be a way of life.

Forgiveness is a practice that we can learn to apply in every area of our lives. Lack of forgiveness makes us - not the offender - ugly in the heart. To forgive perpetually is to be in a state of perpetual peace.

Yes, we sometimes must stand up for ourselves, and yes, we must create a sensible boundary between ourselves and an offending person. And yes, people need to be held to account.

But the secret of forgiveness is to respond to people from a place of internal peace, rather than from a place of anger, righteousness, indignation, annoyance, or whatever emotion may be present.

We can make tragedy make sense when we allow it to help us find our way back to each other and to God's grace.

It can be painful, but not as painful as resisting God's love.

I hope that you long to be free and at peace at this very moment.

Don't practice forgiveness later; practice forgiveness now. I don't care who it is that has hurt you. God can heal you. Not later, but now. All of us need to take a regular inventory of our resentments.

We CAN arrive at a place of total, unconditional forgiveness of ourselves, our pastors, our bosses, our irritating co-workers, our children, our spouses.

Forgiveness can become a daily practice. It can become a constant attitude.

I want you to close your eyes for a few moments and visualize the person in your life you are having difficulty forgiving.

Now, keeping your eyes closed, I want you to imagine yourself being physically raised above that person at the same physical distance Christ was raised up above his persecutors on the cross. You are up on the cross and Christ is there with you.

Look down at the crowd. Look down at that person you cannot forgive.

From the vantage point of the cross, can you see how LOST your tormentor is? Can you see how human he is? Can you see how tortured she is with her own personal demons? Can you picture your own face down there in that same crowd?

Christ was physically raised ABOVE the people who were crucifying him. His love was so great, their rage and violence were something to pity. Their pettiness and spite did not even occupy the same space as His love.

We, all of us, get to live in the space of love...where the violence and sin of others can be something to pity, something that needs to be healed.

What does it take to live above the hurts and in the freedom of forgiveness? Love like Christ.

How do you find this love? Many of us experience it first through the love of people.

Were you ever loved unconditionally by a person when you felt completely unlovable? This is how Christ loves.

When we forgive, we live in a small way like Christ, for we do as he did. It is a spiritual act. With it, we gain healing and freedom.

"Father, forgive them, for they don't know what they are doing." (Luke 23:34)

Choosing to Rise

"To err is human, to forgive divine."

This powerful little quote is attributed to English poet Alexander Pope (1688-1744). Why is extending forgiveness so difficult? Ask God to give you that divine forgiveness demonstrated on the cross by Jesus. Take some time to consider all the ways God and others have extended their hand of forgiveness to you.

CHAPTER 5

MOVING IN A DIFFERENT DIRECTION

"Comebacks don't seem likely when your back is up against the wall and your hope is depleted. But if you will stay the course, you will discover God's power to reverse the irreversible in your life." - Tony Evans

I first committed my life to Jesus in college. I told my rock band at the time that I went to Bible college. They all thought I was a nut. And I was. A nut for Jesus.

I ended up attending Gulf Coast Bible College, where I met my first wife. And for over 30 years, I served the Lord as a pastor and it was a wonderful time.

However, prior to the brain injury, my life was spinning out of control. I had been living a wrong life. I had not been living for the Lord, but living for myself. I was not a good person.

I was not only unfaithful to my first wife but my second wife as well. For several years, I was living a selfish life.

The brain injury helped me to find a new direction towards God and a better way of life. I realized that without God, I would have been without hope and helpless.

I have been born again, "again."

I believe God is number one and He is the One who gives me inspiration and hope for living in a positive way.

I cannot take credit for it. It has been given as a gift from God.

Failure and a setback do not have to be the end. It can be the beginning of something new.

A setback does not have to be a permanent stumbling block. But with a setback, you can always have an amazing comeback.

And that is how I look at my life. I have had a significant setback but an even greater comeback.

God is the God of the comeback!

God is my best friend. He never lets me down. A friend will disappoint me sometimes, but never God. He is always inspirational.

He knows it all. He is going to work it out some way. God's Word is the best word and the final word.

Unlike at Burger King, we can't always have it our way. But you can always have it God's way. He is the King of kings.

My comeback would not have been possible without faith in God. I went through a test and now have a testimony.

You can have a terrible tragedy happen but you can always come back. Your setback can be a door to a comeback.

Choosing to Rise

Have you been born again spiritually? If not, ponder the following scriptures before lifting up the prayer that follows if you so choose.

- ",,,for all have sinned and fall short of the glory of God," - Romans 3:23
- "For the wages of sin is death, but the gift of God is eternal life in Christ Jesus our Lord." - Romans 6:23

- "Jesus replied, "Very truly I tell you, no one can see the kingdom of God unless they are born again." - John 3:3
- "Jesus answered, "I am the way and the truth and the life. No one comes to the Father except through me." - John 14:6
- "If you declare with your mouth, "Jesus is Lord," and believe in your heart that God raised him from the dead, you will be saved. For it is with your heart that you believe and are justified, and it is with your mouth that you profess your faith and are saved." - Romans 10:9-10
- "And he died for all, that those who live should no longer live for themselves but for him who died for them and was raised again." - 2 Corinthians 5:15
- "Here I am! I stand at the door and knock. If anyone hears my voice and opens the door, I will come in and eat with that person, and they with me." - Revelation 3:20

Prayer:

Heavenly Father, I have sinned against You. I want forgiveness of all my sins. I believe Jesus died on the cross for me and rose again. Father, I give You my life to do as You wish. I want Jesus Christ to come into my life and into my heart. Make me a new person from the inside out. I ask this in Jesus' name, Amen.

CHAPTER 6

THE ROAD LESS TRAVELED

Jesus looked at them and said, "With man this is impossible, but with God all things are possible." - Matthew 19:26

What would you say if I told you that my ex-wife's husband is now my best friend?

It is amazing, but it's true. Chet is my best friend.

This all came about after my daughters and I agreed it would be best that I transition from Ohio to Florida in March 2021 to live with my younger daughter, Stacey, and her family.

With my ex-wife and her husband, Chet, living only 15 minutes down the road, we would naturally start seeing one another more often.

Most men do not even like their ex-wife's husband and yet I think Chet is a great guy.

We go swimming together at the University of West Florida and we go golfing together.

We also attend the same church. We have attended Bible studies together, where we sit next to each other and attend the same family gatherings.

People cannot believe it! Personally, I would think it was strange.

There are absolutely no weird feelings between me and Chet.

Chet has helped me in many ways. He has given me advice, like making sure I exercise and take a walk every day. I listened to him and have tried to walk in the neighborhood each day.

From Chet's Perspective

My name is Chet and I came into Chuck's life in an unusual way: I married his first wife. During the week of our honeymoon, Chuck was assaulted by an angry young man who knocked Chuck's head into a brick wall. I offered to take my new wife to see him at the rehab hospital, which also allowed her to support her two daughters. She agreed, but suggested we wait until our honeymoon was over.

My visit that weekend allowed me to see, not only how severely he had been assaulted, but to remember how I had allowed myself to be unfaithful years earlier before I accepted Christ at age 31. This helped me to accept Chuck as a part of my wife's family.

Chuck and I just happened to have common interests in golf and swimming, which began to build our friendship. I also became comfortable sitting with him at men's groups and being present with him at family gatherings.

One day I thought about some ways that I could encourage him: challenging him to take walks, to read and study the bible, and to eat healthy (even to try giving up sugar).

Throughout this growing relationship with him, I was able to personally witness his positive attitude. I saw how he had made a comeback from a challenging situation that would now be permanent. It may seem odd to others that we are friends; but when I hear Chuck say, "Chet is my best friend" (in a way that only he can say it), I smile. That's because only God can do the impossible!

Accept what IS, let go of what WAS, and enjoy what WILL BE.

Choosing to Rise

Have you ever experienced something that you never thought possible? Ask God to help you reach out to someone you have had difficulty with in the past.

CONCLUSION

"Faith sees the invisible, believes the unbelievable, and receives the impossible." - Corrie Ten Boom

Most people see my injury as a tragedy, but for me, it has created an opportunity to love more deeply. Strange as it sounds, I see my brain injury as a great gift.

People think I'm special to have forgiven this man, but trust me, I am not an abnormally good person. What is true, however, is that the path of forgiveness can take ordinary people on an extraordinary journey.

I walk funny and talk funny and have a thousand impairments. Some are visible and some are invisible.

But I'm still exactly who I was made to be, doing exactly what I was born to do, saying exactly what I was born to say.

One of the greatest joys is when this life of mine, which includes my brain injury, can inspire others. I probably wouldn't have arrived at such a surprising way of life without a knock to my head.

But I'm glad to be in a place where I can highly recommend it to you. Not the knock to the head, but this new, surprising way of life.

DISCUSSION GUIDE

Chapter One:

1. What were some initial emotions you felt while reading about Dr. Sandstrom's assault and its aftermath?
2. How can being "knocked down" be a catalyst for transformation or growth?
3. How do you typically react when faced with unexpected and severe difficulties?
4. Why do you think the author emphasized he lived through the experience rather than focusing on the tragedy of it?
5. Describe an event in your life that included a long recovery, whether physically, emotionally, mentally, or spiritually.

Chapter Two:

1. Describe what it means to you to have a bounce back mindset in life?
2. How does Dr. Sandstrom's journey inspire you to face your own challenges?
3. Can you think of a time in your life when you had to adapt to a "Bounce Back Mindset"?

4. What role does gratitude play in your own life and how can it contribute to resilience?

5. Who in your life has helped you bounce back from a difficult circumstance? Consider reaching out to them this week with a phone call, text, email, or letter to let them know how grateful you are for them. Let us know next week how it goes.

Chapter Three:

1. Check In: Did you reach out to one person who has helped you bounce back? If so, how did it go?

2. How can you help someone you know stand back up after they have been knocked down?

3. When you think of a timeline of your life, what are some dates or experiences that most shaped who you are today?

4. What strategies or methods do you use to stand back up after a setback?

5. What are some lessons that you have learned from your own experiences of standing back up?

Chapter Four:

1. How does Dr. Sandstrom's act of forgiveness challenge or confirm your own beliefs about forgiveness?

2. How does forgiveness contribute to personal growth and healing according to this chapter?

3. Why do you think forgiveness is so difficult for us?

4. Can you share a personal experience in the past where forgiveness played a vital role?

5. "But if you do not forgive others their sins, your Father will not forgive your sins." - Matthew 6:15. Considering this verse, ask your Heavenly Father to bring to mind anyone you've been "holding hostage" with resentment and unforgiveness before taking the courageous step of extending forgiveness to them.

Chapter Five:

1. How does faith play a role in the decisions Dr. Sandstrom made in his life after the attack?

2. What kind of impact do you think Dr. Sandstrom's new direction might have had on those around him?

3. Can you discuss a time in your life when you had to move in a different direction?

4. How does Dr. Sandstrom's move in a different direction inspire you to make changes in your own life?

5. Read the story of the Prodigal Son in Luke 15:11-32. How can you allow God to turn your setbacks

into comebacks? Your tragedies into triumphs? Are you able to return home to a Heavenly Father waiting with open arms?

Chapter Six:

1. How do you interpret the quote by Corrie Ten Boom in the context of your own life experiences? "Faith sees the invisible, believes the unbelievable, and receives the impossible."
2. Share a personal experience where you saw the invisible, believed the unbelievable, and received the impossible.
3. How has reading Dr. Sandstrom's story impacted your viewpoint on overcoming adversities?
4. How can you apply the lessons learned from Dr. Sandstrom's journey in your own life?
5. Are you facing something that seems impossible? Perhaps the mending of a broken relationship? A financial crisis? A health issue? In a journal or notebook, pour out your heart to God and ask Him to do what only He can do. Ask Him to grant you patience as you wait for Him to move in your situation.

ABOUT THE AUTHOR

Dr. Chuck Sandstrom has experience as a seasoned organizational leader with over 30 years' experience as a pastor and most recently, the executive director of a community foundation. In 2009, he was brutally assaulted by a stranger. As an author and TEDx speaker, his mission in life is to inspire others through his story.

In this book, he shares how despite his life-altering catastrophic brain injury, he unconditionally forgave the man who assaulted him and began actively engaging in assisting the man's young family. He learned how to bounce back.

www.ingramcontent.com/pod-product-compliance
Lightning Source LLC
Chambersburg PA
CBHW060544030426
42337CB00021B/4427